This book belongs to:

_____

Contents

Ladybird

Cover illustration by Amanda Wood

Published by Ladybird Books Ltd
27 Wrights Lane London W8 5TZ
A Penguin Company

2 4 6 8 10 9 7 5 3 1

© LADYBIRD BOOKS LTD MCMXCVII, MMI

Printed in Italy

Fingers in the yogurts

written by Marie Birkinshaw

illustrated by Serena Feneziani

Dad had been shopping.

4

We all helped to put
the things away.

Tom put the bananas
in the fruit basket.

Sally put the cheese
in the fridge.

Dad put the chocolate
on the top shelf.

Sarah put her fingers
in the yogurts and...

we were **all** put outside!

Under the sky

written by Lorraine Horsley

illustrated by Amanda Wood

Under the sky is the sun.

Under the sun is a tree.

Under the tree is a branch.

Under the branch is me.

Under me is a rock.

Under the rock is the ground.

Under the ground
   is a big pink worm...

Wriggling and squiggling
   around.

Nina's new puppy

written by Marie Birkinshaw

illustrated by Julie Anderson

Nina and her family had
a new puppy.

First the puppy chewed
Dad's boots.
Nina laughed.

Then the puppy chewed
Mum's gloves. Nina
laughed again.

But when the puppy chewed Nina's books, Nina didn't laugh. Nina was cross.

And when the puppy
chewed Nina's **rabbit**,

Nina was so cross that she went back to the shop...

Now Nina's puppy has
something of his **own**
to chew.

Beaker Squeaker

written by Shirley Jackson
illustrated by David Mostyn

Beaker Squeaker
sat on a wall.

Beaker Squeaker
had a red ball.

Beaker Squeaker
ran over the chairs.

Beaker Squeaker
ran down the stairs.

Beaker Squeaker
ran over the floor.

Beaker Squeaker
ran round the door.

Beaker Squeaker
went out through her flap.

Beaker Squeaker
went for a nap.

Beaker Squeaker

Read the first line of this rhyme to your child and
encourage her to read the rest to you, with your help.
Can she point to the words that rhyme? See if you
can read it together a little quicker each time.

Does Beaker Squeaker remind you
of a nursery rhyme?

New words

Encourage your child to use some
of these new words to help her
to write her own very simple
stories and rhymes.

One or two sentences is great.
Go back to look at earlier books
and their wordlists to practise
other words.

Read with Ladybird

Read with Ladybird has been written to help you to help your child:

- to take the first steps in reading
- to improve early reading progress
- to gain confidence

Main Features

- **Several stories and rhymes in each book**

This means that there is not too much for you and your child to read in one go.

- **Rhyme and rhythm**

Read with Ladybird uses rhymes or stories with a rhythm to help your child to predict and memorise new words.

- **Gradual introduction and repetition of key words**

Read with Ladybird introduces and repeats the 100 most frequently used words in the English language.

- **Compatible with school reading schemes**

The key words that your child will learn are compatible with the word lists that are used in schools. This means that you can be confident that practising at home will support work done at school.

- **Information pullout**

Use this pullout to understand more about how you can use each story to help your child to learn to read.

But the most important feature of **Read with Ladybird** is for you and your child to have fun sharing the stories and rhymes with each other.

Learning to read with this book

Fingers in the yogurts

Would your child like to try to read this story to you – with your help? Take time to enjoy the pictures and help her with any word she does not know. Encourage her to read the story again, and to enjoy the feeling of fluency.

Under the sky

Encourage your child to read this rhyme to you. Help her to use pictures and the first letters and sounds of the words to read those words that are new to her. Also, ask her what she thinks the words are likely to be. Suggest that she go back and re-read the complete sentence that contains a newly learnt or corrected word.

Nina's new puppy

How would your child like you to help her? Would she like you to read the story to her first, or would she prefer to attempt it on her own? Encourage her to look for letters and sounds at the ends of words – ple, the past tense verbs chew**ed**, This shows her that reading the d is important.